For Anna, who helped me uncover
The Brave Lisa.
—LK

For Willow, with all my love.
—HG

Author's Note

This story is about being brave when you are trying something for the first time and about what kids can do when they feel scared. But guess what? Grown-ups get scared too! Including me.

Let me tell you about where I got the idea for this story. I was talking to a therapist, which is a person whose job is to help you understand and manage your feelings. You might have a social worker or counselor at your school who helps with this kind of thing.

I was telling my therapist about how I get super nervous before I teach a writing class or give a presentation. My tummy feels all tied up in knots and I can't even eat my breakfast! Sometimes my hands get shaky, and I worry that I will mess up, or not be good enough.

But, once I start teaching my class or giving my presentation, I realize that something takes over. After I get past my first wave of nerves, I am fine. Once I start talking or teaching, I feel awesome.

When I shared this with my therapist, she told me that I was The Brave Lisa in those moments. The Brave Lisa is a part of me that is always there but might be hidden beneath worry or doubt. Then she asked me to do something grown-ups don't do too much, but kids do all the time. She asked me to pretend!

She suggested that when I am feeling scared and my tummy is all mixed-up, I should remember those great moments when I am The Brave Lisa and pretend to be her. The first time I tried it, I felt kind of silly. But I gave it a shot and pictured myself being brave. And you know what? My tummy didn't feel as wild as it usually does. My hands were not as shaky. I was still nervous the first few times I pretended to be The Brave Lisa, but not as much.

And after trying lots of times, something changed. When I started doing a scary thing, like teaching a roomful of grown-ups, The Brave Lisa was ready to go! I sailed through those nervous moments and got right to the fun part of teaching.

I still work on finding The Brave Lisa. Some days I need to start by pretending. Some days she is already there. But now I know how to tap into The Brave Lisa whenever I need to.

I hope this story helps you find The Brave You inside yourself. Don't forget, it has always been there and always will be.

Lisa

I CAN DO IT
Even If I'm Scared

FINDING THE BRAVE YOU

Words by
Lisa Katzenberger

sourcebooks
eXplore

Pictures by
Hannah George

Trying something new can bring up lots of feelings. Maybe, on the outside, you look excited for an adventure, ready to dive right in.

But on the inside…

your tummy tumbles

and your heart hiccups

and your fingers fiddle.

Maybe, deep down,
you're kind of scared.

Did you know there's a way to be brave in these moments?
To feel strong enough to face your fears.
Bold enough to try anything.

There's even someone who can help:
The Brave You.

Who is The Brave You? It's a strong and bold part of you deep inside.
A part of you that can make the impossible possible.

But how do you find The Brave You?

First, imagine yourself as The Brave You.
Go on and picture them in your mind.

Take a deep breath.
Close your eyes if it helps.
Want to peek?
That's okay too.

Ask a few questions.

What does The Brave You look like?

What does The Brave You feel like?

What does The Brave You sound like?

Hold on tight to that picture.

Next, play pretend and watch what happens. How does The Brave You act? What does The Brave You say? What does The Brave You see?

Pretend as much as you need. As long as you want.
Over and over. Again and again.

Something is shifting inside of you. Do you feel it?
Good. You are growing, stretching, changing.

Now, this last step is a big one. Ready?

Act like you are The Brave You in real life.

Do something that scares you.

Don't forget, The Brave You is doing the hard work.

Remember how The Brave You acted when it was just pretend? Do that.

You can start small. Lots of little steps add up to one large leap.

Are you still scared? That's okay.
This is a big job.
But you've got this.

Go ahead and give it a shot.

You might not get it right
the first time.
That's OK. Keep trying,
until you can say—

Wow! I did it!

How did that feel? Pretty amazing, right?

Then after you've pictured The Brave You,
pretended to be The Brave You,
even acted as The Brave You,
there is one last tip to share.

One day, The Brave You won't be a different version of yourself—it will become your whole self. You won't have to picture and practice and pretend. You will be able to face your fear without even thinking about it.

And then you might wonder, is this brave person really me?

Yes.

It is you.

It is you.

It is you.

It always was.

　　And it always will be.

Feeling a Little Scared? Try This!

Everyone—including grown-ups—gets scared at times. It's a natural human emotion. But we can learn to manage that feeling so it's not overpowering, and it doesn't prevent us from trying something new. Here is an activity you can do with a friend or trusted adult to find The Brave You.

- Think about a time in the past when you were scared. Either scared of something that had already happened, or scared of something that might happen. Talk about it or draw a picture of it.

- Now, think about that time you were scared in the past. Ask yourself: Did you survive it to be here today? Yes, you did!

- Next, ask yourself if there is something that hasn't happened yet that you are scared of or worried about. It's OK to admit it. Talking about our fears is the first step to making them less powerful. Talk about it or draw a picture of it.

- Now, remembering that you have been brave in the past and made it through scary moments, think about how you would want to act the next time you feel scared about something. Talk about it or draw a picture of it.

Now you have a plan to follow the next time you get scared. With this plan, The Brave You will shine through and remind you just how strong you really are.

A message to parents, guardians, and caregivers from Heather Davidson, Psy.D, BCN

Most parents would agree that they want what's best for their child, but what exactly is the best response to your child's fear? When your child is in distress—frightened, crying—a parent's first instinct is likely to offer comfort and reassurance. However, when you're dealing with a fearful child, reassuring them can fuel their worries rather than soothe them. A fearful child will feed off your reassurance to the point that they believe they must receive a steady stream of it in order to stay safe.

However, as a parent, you don't want to completely ignore your child's distress, so it can be a tricky balancing act. How can you be supportive without inadvertently feeding your child's fear? One way is by talking through the problem with them. Providing your child with the opportunity to explore their thoughts and emotions without necessarily reassuring them can increase distress tolerance and self-confidence. Another way is by helping them identify coping strategies they can use in a stressful situation.

You don't need to remove them or tell them exactly what to do, but you absolutely can remind them about coping strategies they've learned or ask them which of several tactics might work best given the situation and how they're feeling. This facilitates cognitive growth, independence, and self-confidence.

Does Your Child Need More Support?

At what point does my child's fear indicate a need for professional help? What does professional help look like? Won't my child be stigmatized if I get them professional help?

It really comes down to your child's level of distress and functioning. Are they refusing school, failing classes, in distress more often throughout the day than they are not in distress? If you answered yes to any of those questions, it may be time to get outside support. Many parents fear they'll be viewed as a failure if they seek professional help, but in fact it takes strength and courage to acknowledge when you need support. A therapist's goal is not to "fix" your child, but to teach a parent, a child, and the family unit the best way to overcome a problem by working together.

If you feel your family would benefit from professional support, search online for licensed therapists in your community, or ask your medical provider how to get a referral.

Take a deep breath and remind yourself that you're doing the very best you can. Being a parent is hard, and it's even harder when you have a child struggling with overwhelming fear. It's not easy to admit there's a problem, and it's not easy to do the work needed to change. You're learning new strategies that your child can implement, but you're also learning new strategies you can use yourself.

DR. HEATHER DAVIDSON, Psy.D, BCN, is a New York State–licensed child psychologist. Dr. Davidson received her master's and doctoral degrees from The Chicago School of Professional Psychology. She holds certifications from Columbia University and the Albert Ellis Institute in cognitive behavioral therapy (CBT) and rational emotive behavior therapy (REBT).

The message to parents was originally published, in a different
form, in *CBT Workbook for Kids* by Heather Davidson Psy.D BCN.

The characters and events portrayed in this book are fictitious
or are used fictitiously. Any similarity to real persons, living or
dead, is purely coincidental and not intended by the author.

The full color art was created using Procreate on an iPad Pro.

Published by Sourcebooks eXplore, an imprint
of Sourcebooks Kids
P.O. Box 4410, Naperville, Illinois 60567-4410
(630) 961-3900
sourcebookskids.com

Cataloging-in-Publication Data is on file with the
Library of Congress.

Source of Production: Toppan Leefung Printing Ltd.,
Dongguan, Guangdong Province, China
Date of Production: February 2024
Run Number: 5037415

Printed and bound in China.
TL 10 9 8 7 6 5 4 3 2 1